W9-BBC-578

DISCARD

THE OJIBWE

BY MICHELLE LEVINE

CONSULTANT: JILL DOERFLER
WHITE EARTH OJIBWE
PH.D. CANDIDATE
AMERICAN STUDIES
UNIVERSITY OF MINNESOTA

LERNER PUBLICATIONS
MINNEAPOLIS

ABOUT THE COVER IMAGE: This shoulder bag, or bandolier, from 1900 is decorated with a traditional Ojibwe floral design.

NOTE: There are various spellings for the name *Ojibwe*. Some of these include Ojibwa and Ojibway.

PHOTO ACKNOWLEDGMENTS:
The images in this book are used with the permission of: Peabody Museum, Harvard University, Photo 995-29-10/73205A T2111, pp. 1, 3, 4, 18, 28, 42; Charles Lanman, Minnesota Historical Society, p. 5; Agricultural Research Service, USDA, p. 6; Library of Congress, pp. 7 (LC-USZC4-7312), 19 (LC-USZ62-60814), 27 (LC-USZ62-105740), 37 (LC-DIG-cwpbh-01769); Wisconsin Historical Society, pp. 8 (6912), 17 (35217), 24 (2103), 32 (35051), 33 (1900), 39 (23888); Minnesota Historical Society, pp. 9, 12, 25, 38, 40; U.S. Fish and Wildlife Service, p. 10; © Marilyn "Angel" Wynn/Nativestock.com, pp. 13, 26, 49; © North Wind Picture Archives, pp. 14, 29, 35; © Raymond Gehman/CORBIS, p. 15; The Bancroft Library, University of California, Berkeley, p. 16; Ulysses S. Cox, Minnesota Historical Society, p. 21; General Research Division, The New York Public Library, p. 22; Neg. no. 320374, Courtesy Department of Library Services, American Museum of Natural History, p. 23; © CORBIS, p. 31; Seth Eastman, Minnesota Historical Society, p. 34; Bernard Freemont Childs, Minnesota Historical Society, p. 36; © Raymond Bial, pp. 43, 45, 46, 50; © Bettmann/CORBIS, p. 44; © Keri Pickett, image courtesy of South End Press, p. 47; Michael Dorris/Henry Holt and Co., p. 48; © Erica Johnson/Independent Picture Service, p. 51. Cover: Minnesota Historical Society.

Lerner Publications Company
A division of Lerner Publishing Group
241 First Avenue North
Minneapolis, MN 55401 U.S.A.

Website address: www.lernerbooks.com

Library of Congress Cataloging-in-Publication Data

Levine, Michelle.
    The Ojibwe / by Michelle Levine.
        p.   cm. — (Native American histories)
    Includes bibliographical references and index.
    ISBN-13: 978-0-8225-5910-8 (lib. bdg. : alk. paper)
    ISBN-10: 0-8225-5910-2 (lib. bdg. : alk. paper)
    1. Ojibwa Indians—History. 2. Ojibwa Indians—Social life and customs.
3. Ojibwa Indians—Religion. I. Title. II. Series.
E99.C6L43 2007
977.004'97333—dc22   2005024008

Manufactured in the United States of America
1 2 3 4 5 6 – BP – 12 11 10 09 08 07

CONTENTS

CHAPTER 1

BEGINNINGS

THE OJIBWE ARE NATIVE PEOPLE OF NORTH AMERICA.

This continent is their original homeland. Native North Americans are called American Indians or Native Americans. The Ojibwe call themselves the Anishinabe. This word means "original people." The name *Ojibwe* may have come from their American Indian neighbors.

The Ojibwe probably once lived near the Atlantic Ocean in modern-day Canada. They began moving westward around six hundred years ago. By the 1500s or 1600s, most Ojibwe had made their way to Lake Superior. This Great Lake is in the northern United States. The Ojibwe lived in forested woodlands near the lake.

Many Ojibwe settled on the land around Lake Superior.

Many deer lived in the Ojibwe's new, wooded homeland.

The Ojibwe's new home was rich with plant and animal life. Trees, such as maple, birch, and pine, grew in tall clusters. Wild berry bushes had sweet fruits. Animals, such as bears, deer, porcupines, and wild birds, lived in the woods. Fish filled Lake Superior and nearby rivers and streams. And tasty wild rice grew in watery fields.

BANDS AND CLANS

The Ojibwe people shared many traditions. They also spoke a common language. But they did not have a single leader. Instead, they lived in separate groups called bands. Bands often were made up of three hundred to four hundred people. They included several extended families.

Each band had a chief. The chief helped lead when needed. The chief had the help of a council. A council is a group of respected community members.

Together, the chief and council led the band in many ways. They settled arguments between band members. They gave families rights to certain hunting and fishing areas. And they chose punishments for people who had caused harm to others.

This is the Ojibwe chief Pee-Che-Kir. He helped lead his community in the 1800s.

The Ojibwe often lived together in large family groups.

Each Ojibwe also belonged to a group called a clan. The Ojibwe word for "clan" is *dodaim,* or totem. Each dodaim was made up of people who shared the same ancestors. An Ojibwe person belonged to the dodaim of his or her father. Dodaim members thought of one another as relatives. They did not marry one another. Members of each dodaim were spread out among the Ojibwe bands.

The main clans among the Ojibwe people were the crane, catfish, bear, marten, wolf, and loon dodaim. But there were many other smaller dodaim. Each dodaim played a certain role in society. For example, leaders often came from the crane dodaim. Teachers and storytellers often belonged to the catfish dodaim. Clans remain an important part of modern Ojibwe culture.

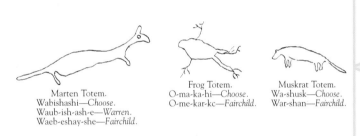

Marten Totem.
Wabishashi—*Choose*.
Waub-ish-ash-e—*Warren*.
Waeb-eshay-she—*Fairchild*.

Frog Totem.
O-ma-ka-hi—*Choose*.
O-me-kar-kc—*Fairchild*.

Muskrat Totem.
Wa-shusk—*Choose*.
War-shan—*Fairchild*.

Each dodaim had its own symbol.

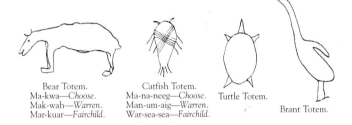

Bear Totem.
Ma-kwa—*Choose*.
Mak-wah—*Warren*.
Mar-kuar—*Fairchild*.

Catfish Totem.
Ma-na-neeg—*Choose*.
Man-um-aig—*Warren*.
War-sea-sea—*Fairchild*.

Turtle Totem.

Brant Totem.

Sucker Totem.

Duck Totem or Cormorant Totem.
She-sheb—*Choose*.
Muk-ud-a-shib—*Warren*.
She-sheb—*Fairchild*.

TOTEM SIGNS OF THE OJIBWA.

THE GREAT MYSTERY

The Ojibwe believed in a Great Spirit, or God. They called this spirit Kitche Manitou. This name means the "Creator," or the "Great Spirit." Kitche Manitou made everything on Earth. He sent other spirits, or manitous, to care for his creations. Every kind of animal had its own manitou. Even rocks and trees had manitous. The Ojibwe always tried to live in peace with the manitous. They did not want to upset a spirit by hurting any part of nature.

Animals are sacred in the Ojibwe religion. This animal is a marten. An Ojibwe dodaim is named after the marten.

A SECOND CREATION

One Ojibwe legend tells of a great flood. The story says it happened some time after Kitche Manitou created Earth. A deep sea covered all the land. A spirit being named Sky Woman lived all alone above the sea. One day, the water animals invited Sky Woman to live with them. A giant turtle rose to the top of the water. Sky Woman came down to rest on its back. Then she asked the water animals to get some mud from the sea's bottom. The muskrat dove down and brought up a small pawful of mud. The woman put the mud on the turtle's back. Then she breathed life into it. The mud grew and grew until it became North America. After that, Sky Woman gave birth to twins, a boy and a girl. This birth led to the beginnings of the Ojibwe people.

Many Ojibwe gathered for thanksgiving ceremonies at least twice each year. The ceremonies honored Kitche Manitou. They were special times to give thanks to the Creator and other manitous. These also were times to offer prayers and ask for help.

These Ojibwe in Red Lake, Minnesota, are dancing at a ceremony called a powwow.

The Ojibwe people performed other ceremonies to mark important occasions. They held ceremonies to name children, join couples in marriage, and honor people who had died.

A sacred pipe was an important part of all ceremonies. The Ojibwe used this pipe to communicate with the spirits. They believed that rising pipe smoke would help their prayers reach the manitous. Modern Ojibwe still honor Kitche Manitou. They respect the manitous and try to please them with their actions.

This ceremonial pipe is from the Great Lakes area.

Spending time alone outdoors was an important part of a vision quest.

VISION QUEST

When an Ojibwe child turned about twelve years old, the child often went on a vision quest. Just before the vision quest, the child's parent or grandparent would build a simple shelter far away from the village. The child would go to the shelter to pray and fast for about four days. *Fast* means "to not eat."

During this time, the child would usually hear a voice or see a vision. But sometimes a child needed to go on more than one quest to see a vision. When the vision appeared, the child could see his or her guardian spirit. This spirit promised to offer advice, knowledge, and wisdom to the child. Some Ojibwe still go on vision quests. The quests help them feel connected to the spirit world.

A young person might create a reminder of the vision. It might look like one of these rock paintings of a human figure *(upper left)*, a small mammal *(lower left)*, and a moose *(right)*.

SICKNESS OF THE SPIRIT

The Ojibwe believed that illness was connected to a person's soul or spirit. They had different ways of curing illnesses. A sick person might go to the village sweat lodge. Sweat lodges were full of heat and steam. The Ojibwe believed that heat and steam could heal the body and spirit.

American Indians plunge into a cool river after sitting in a steamy sweat lodge *(far right)*.

An Ojibwe healer prepares a medicine to cure a sick patient. Singing and shaking a rattle are rituals that are parts of this important task.

For more serious illnesses, a person might go to a medicine man or woman. These healers used prayers, rituals, and charms. They also used medicines made from plants. Medicine men and women believed that bad actions caused many illnesses. They tried to live good lives by treating nature and their fellow people with respect. They encouraged the members of their communities to live good lives too. In modern times, many Ojibwe see medical doctors when they are ill. They also sometimes go to Ojibwe healers.

CHAPTER 2

OJIBWE LIFEWAYS

FOR PART OF THE YEAR, OJIBWE PEOPLE LIVED IN VILLAGES. Most villages were made of ten or more families in the same band. The villages were usually near water. Being near water made it easy to fish, farm, and travel. Villagers usually lived in dome-shaped homes. They called the homes wigwams. About eight people could fit in a wigwam. Children, parents, and grandparents often lived together.

An Ojibwe person built a wigwam out of a wooden frame. Then it was covered with strips of bark. Inside the wigwam burned a fire. The fire was for heating the home and cooking food. A hole in the roof let out the fire's smoke. Straw mats covered the floor. Families rolled fur blankets against the walls and used them for sitting. At night, families spread the blankets out on the floor for sleeping.

To build their homes, the Ojibwe made frames from wood. Next, they covered the frames with bark from trees.

FAR AND WIDE

In the woodlands, the Ojibwe grew in number and in strength through the years. They spread over larger and larger areas of land. Most Ojibwe stayed in the woodlands of upper North America. But one group of Ojibwe moved farther west. They were called the Bungee. The Bungee ended up on the Great Plains of North Dakota and Montana. They lived very differently from the Ojibwe of the woodlands. Like other Plains Indians, these Ojibwe were nomadic. They traveled from place to place. They lived in tipis instead of wigwams. On the plains, the Bungee followed and hunted the American bison.

GROWING UP OJIBWE

Young children stayed close to home. Their parents, aunts, uncles, and grandparents took care of them. At around the age of seven, children began to do chores.

An Ojibwe girl and baby in a cradleboard pose for a photo in 1901. Ojibwe families used cradleboards to carry their babies. Some families lived in bark-covered tipis such as this one.

Boys set out with the men in their village. They learned how to make canoes from cedarwood and birch bark. They practiced fishing with woven nets. They also studied the ways of the woods and the animals. They learned how to set traps. The Ojibwe trapped animals for their meat. Boys learned how to use bows and arrows too. When a boy hunted his first animal, the entire village celebrated with a big feast.

An Ojibwe girl helps cook a meal over an outdoor fire.

Girls learned how to run a household and take care of younger children. They helped the women plant and pick corn and other crops. They learned to gather wild plants and berries for food and medicine. Girls also learned how to clean and how to cook meat and other foods. The women taught them how to weave fishing nets and make pottery and birch bark containers. They showed them how to make clothing from animal skins too.

RICE GATHERERS

The Ojibwe lived in their villages during the warm summer months. They used that time to hunt and fish. They also planted crops and gathered berries. When summer ended, families left their homes for many months.

In the fall, the Ojibwe traveled to nearby wild rice fields. There they gathered rice. One person used a long pole to push a canoe through the swampy rice fields. Another person in the canoe bent the rice plants over the edge of the canoe. Then that person used a specially carved stick to knock the rice kernels into the boat.

Gathering rice by hand is a difficult job.
The Ojibwe in modern times still harvest rice by hand.

Families took canoes full of rice back to shore. They dried the rice on warm birch bark strips or flat rocks. They replanted some of the rice harvest for the next year. They would eat the rest of the rice throughout the year.

Winter in the woodlands was cold and harsh. People spent many hours indoors. Men used the winter months to make and repair snowshoes, build animal traps, and repair canoes and other items. They also braved the cold, snowy weather to go hunting.

The Ojibwe wore large wooden snowshoes when they hunted in the winter. The shoes made it easier to walk in high drifts of snow.

This young woman is dressed in warm winter clothes.

Women used the time to weave fishing nets. They also made straw mats and birch bark containers. They sewed and mended clothing too. The Ojibwe wore outfits made of deerskin. In winter, they wore heavy fur coats and moccasins. These shoes had rabbit-fur linings.

Winter evenings were a good time for storytelling. Storytellers told legends about the creation of Earth and the manitous. They also told stories about the heroes of the past. Most stories had hidden lessons about how to be a good person.

In one story, the half-human and half-spirit Nanaboozhoo shows the Ojibwe how to make arrows.

Many stories were about Nanaboozhoo. Nanaboozhoo was half human and half spirit. He was a hero to the Ojibwe people. He helped his people in many ways. In one popular story, Nanaboozhoo discovered wild rice. Other stories told how he taught the Ojibwe people important skills. He showed them how to make canoes, snowshoes, and bows and arrows. He always meant well. But sometimes he made mistakes. The Ojibwe still look to Nanaboozhoo for lessons on how to live good lives.

SUGARING SEASON

In late March and early April, each family left the winter camp. They made their way to a grove of maple trees. Family members worked together to collect the trees' sweet sap. They made holes in the trunks of maple trees. The sap dripped from the trees into birch bark buckets. Once the families had collected the sap, women boiled it in big containers made of animal skin. The sap boiled day and night. It thickened into a sticky syrup. The Ojibwe used the syrup to make sugar for cooking. Once this sugaring season ended, families returned to their villages for the summer.

A woman puts out buckets to collect sap from maple trees.

CHAPTER 3

THE EUROPEANS ARRIVE

THE OJIBWE PEOPLE DID NOT SEE EUROPEANS UNTIL THE 1600s.

By then, French people had come to the woodlands around Lake Superior. The French had a different way of saying the word *Ojibwe*. They pronounced it *Chippewa*. Most of the French people in the woodlands were trappers. These men trapped animals for their fur. Europeans used fur to make fancy clothing. Fur sold for high prices back in Europe.

The French trappers and the Ojibwe had a mostly friendly relationship. Many Frenchmen married Ojibwe women and lived with the Ojibwe people. French trappers also traded with the Ojibwe. In exchange for fur, an Ojibwe hunter could buy European goods. These goods included guns, metal tools, traps, kettles, needles, blankets, and clothing. Many Ojibwe began using European items instead of traditional tools, weapons, and clothing. Over time, they began to depend on the fur trade to survive.

American Indians bring furs to European traders.

THE GRAND MEDICINE SOCIETY

French trappers were not the only Europeans to come to the Ojibwe homeland. Missionaries arrived around the same time. These religious Europeans wanted the Ojibwe people to follow the Christian religion. Some Ojibwe did become Christians.

But many others did not. Some Ojibwe wanted to protect their own customs. They formed a religious organization called the Midéwiwin, or the Grand Medicine Society. Religious leaders, called Midé, were carefully chosen. The Ojibwe believed that the Midé had great spiritual and healing powers. The Midéwiwin still is a powerful religious society in modern times.

THE FIGHT FOR HUNTING GROUNDS

Other Native Americans also traded with the fur trappers. They too had started hunting animals for their fur. Soon there were fewer animals left to hunt.

In the 1600s, an Indian group called the Iroquois fought with the Ojibwe. They fought over hunting grounds. The Ojibwe were peaceful people. But they could be warriors when needed. They protected their villages from attacks. They also fought off the Iroquois to keep control of their land.

The Ojibwe could be fierce warriors. These Ojibwe warriors are performing a dance.

In the 1700s, the Ojibwe began moving farther west. They were looking for new hunting grounds. They took over land in modern-day Michigan, Wisconsin, and Minnesota. Along the way, they fought with the Dakota, Lakota, and Nakota. They also fought the Fox, or Mesquakie, Indians. These other Native Americans already lived on this land. The Ojibwe became one of the most powerful tribes in the area.

Europeans moved to the Ojibwe homeland. This forced the Ojibwe to move west. The Ojibwe fought the Dakota for land in Wisconsin.

The French and Indian War was between the French and the British. Many American Indians fought for the French. Frenchman Charles Langlade *(left)* directs American Indians' attack on the British *(top right)*.

NEW NEIGHBORS

By this time, the French and British were also fighting for control of land in North America. Many Ojibwe sided with the French. They helped the French in battles against the British and their American colonists. Ojibwe warriors fought in the French and Indian War (1754–1763). The British won this war. They gained control of much of the Ojibwe's homeland. The Ojibwe did not trust their new neighbors. They saw that the British did not treat Native Americans with respect.

The American colonists began fighting the British in the Revolutionary War (1775–1783). For years, the king of Great Britain had ruled over the colonists. They were fighting for their freedom. The United States won the war. It became a free nation. The Ojibwe homeland also became part of the United States.

TIME OF THE TREATY

The new U.S. government wanted to trade with the Ojibwe. The U.S. government built many forts. They used these forts as trading centers. The Ojibwe and other Native Americans traveled to the forts to buy and sell goods with white traders.

Fort Snelling *(top left)* is near Saint Paul, Minnesota. The Ojibwe traded there.

In 1815, Ojibwe and other Native American leaders signed a treaty with the United States. A treaty is a written agreement. The treaty said that the United States and the Ojibwe would remain peaceful friends.

But as time passed, things changed. White Americans became interested in the Ojibwe homeland. They wanted to chop down the trees. They said they needed the wood to build homes. They also wanted the land. They planned to use it for farms and homes.

Early European Americans clear the land to build farms and homes.

European Americans illegally took the Ojibwe's traditional homeland.

The Ojibwe would have to go to war with the white Americans to protect their land. Many Ojibwe did not want to fight. Instead, they signed more treaties with the United States. In these treaties, the Ojibwe agreed to sell some of their land.

A large number of Ojibwe agreed to a treaty in 1837. This treaty made an important promise. It said the people could stay on their land. They could still live, hunt, and fish there.

Many white Americans were not happy with the agreement. They did not want to share the land with their Ojibwe neighbors. So the U.S. government broke its promise. It began to force Ojibwe communities off their land.

The U.S. government made Ojibwe people live on smaller pieces of land. These pieces of land were called reservations. In exchange, the government promised to pay the Ojibwe money for their land. They also agreed to give the Ojibwe food, furniture, blankets, and wood for building homes. By the 1860s, most Ojibwe people lived on reservations.

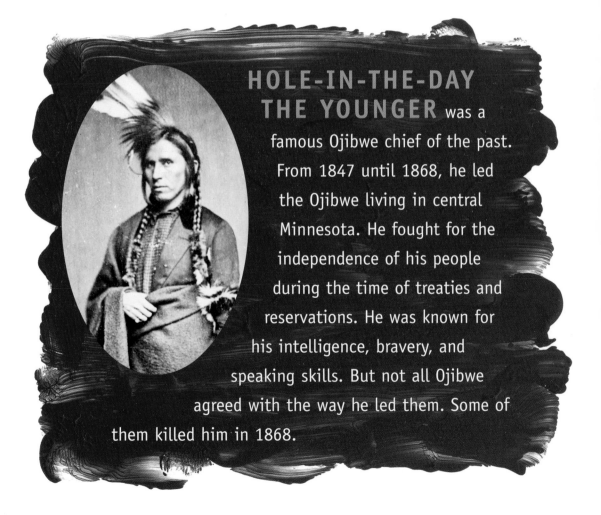

HOLE-IN-THE-DAY THE YOUNGER was a famous Ojibwe chief of the past. From 1847 until 1868, he led the Ojibwe living in central Minnesota. He fought for the independence of his people during the time of treaties and reservations. He was known for his intelligence, bravery, and speaking skills. But not all Ojibwe agreed with the way he led them. Some of them killed him in 1868.

RESERVATION LIFE

Life on the reservation was often hard. Much of the land was not good for hunting or farming. Still, women and children tried to grow crops. Men tried to hunt and fish so their families had enough to eat. Some Ojibwe men found jobs working for companies owned by white people. These Ojibwe worked in places such as mines, mills, and factories.

Even Ojibwe children had to work on farms.

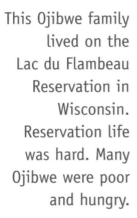

This Ojibwe family lived on the Lac du Flambeau Reservation in Wisconsin. Reservation life was hard. Many Ojibwe were poor and hungry.

Many Ojibwe were very poor. Their homes were small and run-down. They often did not have enough to eat.

Some Ojibwe became sick and died. They caught European diseases, such as smallpox and tuberculosis, a lung disease.

WILLIAM W. WARREN was an Ojibwe writer and lawmaker. In 1851, he became a member of Minnesota's legislature. This government body makes laws for the state. He also wrote articles for the *Minnesota Democrat* newspaper. And he spent time learning about Ojibwe history and traditions from older Ojibwe people. He put his knowledge in a book called *History of the Ojibway People.*

The U.S government did not respect Ojibwe traditions. It wanted the Ojibwe to live like white people. The government expected Ojibwe men to farm for a living. It took away the men's right to hunt and fish on land outside of the reservations. It also made the Ojibwe people stop practicing their religious and cultural traditions.

The U.S. government set up schools for Ojibwe and other Native American children. The children lived at these schools. They had to wear white people's clothes.

The Ojibwe students also had to speak English. Teachers punished the children if they spoke their own language or practiced their traditions. It was a sad time for the Ojibwe people.

Ojibwe students wearing white people's clothes pose with their teachers for a photo at Red Lake School in Red Lake, Minnesota.

CHAPTER 4

LIFE IN MODERN TIMES

IN THE 1900s, THE OJIBWE PEOPLE STRUGGLED TO SURVIVE on the reservations. Many people did not have good health. They had a hard time finding jobs. Although the Ojibwe lived in the United States, they were not U.S. citizens. They did not have the same rights as white people. In 1924, Congress passed a new law. It said that all Native Americans could be U.S. citizens. But the U.S. government still did not give the Ojibwe and other American Indians the same rights as white people.

In the 1960s, the Ojibwe began speaking out for better treatment. They wanted to build their own schools and have their own doctors. They wanted the U.S. government to recognize the Ojibwe as an independent nation. Ojibwe leaders also fought for the right to hunt and fish on their original homeland. New laws returned important rights to the Ojibwe people.

In modern times, the Ojibwe are in charge of their reservations. These tribal offices are on the Mille Lacs reservation in Minnesota.

THE AMERICAN INDIAN MOVEMENT

In 1968, several Ojibwe leaders helped organize the American Indian Movement (AIM). Members of AIM spoke out for the rights of Native Americans. They believed in self-determination. They believed American Indian communities should have the right to take care of themselves. They also believed in returning to the spirituality and values of traditional Native American culture. AIM helped return land to Native American tribes. It also encouraged the U.S. government to support schools, medical clinics, and housing programs run by American Indians. AIM still works for Native American rights in the United States and Canada.

AIM leaders Vernon Bellecourt *(left)* and Dennis Banks *(right)* meet with reporters in 1972. Both are Ojibwe.

A BETTER LIFE

Since the late 1900s and early 2000s, the Ojibwe have been working to make life better on the reservations. Tribal schools teach children about Ojibwe values, traditions, and language. Community centers allow families to gather for Ojibwe classes, ceremonies, and social events. Doctors and Ojibwe healers on reservations keep people healthy.

Reservations also have their own governments. These governments usually have a leader chosen by the people. The leader is called a chairperson, chief, or executive. The leader works with other community leaders. The leader tries to improve life for people on the reservations. The reservations have their own lawmakers, judges, and police officers.

Ojibwe reservations have their own police departments.

The casino at Mille Lacs in Minnesota greatly benefits the Mille Lacs reservation.

Some Ojibwe have also opened casinos. At casinos, people try to win money by playing games. The casinos provide jobs and money for Ojibwe people. They are open to both native and nonnative visitors.

EVERYDAY LIFE

More than 100,000 Ojibwe live in the United States. At least 60,000 others are in Canada. Some of these Native Americans live on reservations. Many reservations are in Montana, North Dakota, Minnesota, Wisconsin, Michigan, and in Ontario, Canada. Other Ojibwe live in towns and cities nearby and throughout North America.

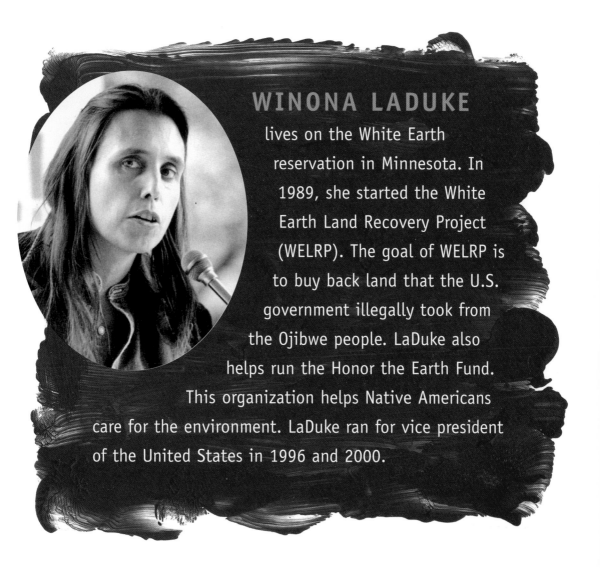

WINONA LADUKE lives on the White Earth reservation in Minnesota. In 1989, she started the White Earth Land Recovery Project (WELRP). The goal of WELRP is to buy back land that the U.S. government illegally took from the Ojibwe people. LaDuke also helps run the Honor the Earth Fund. This organization helps Native Americans care for the environment. LaDuke ran for vice president of the United States in 1996 and 2000.

Ojibwe men and women work in many kinds of jobs. They are teachers, writers, nurses, and doctors. They are farmers, government workers, and business owners. They attend schools, colleges, and universities.

LOUISE ERDRICH is an Ojibwe writer who grew up in a family of storytellers. She has published poetry, stories, and novels. Many of her books are about Ojibwe people living in modern times. Erdrich has won awards and prizes for her writing. Some of her books include *The Beet Queen, The Antelope Wife, The Birchbark House,* and *The Game of Silence.*

Modern Ojibwe people find many ways to honor their traditions. They gather together for powwows. At powwows, many Ojibwe dress in special clothing. They participate in traditional dances and drumming events. Some powwows include competitions. Men, women, and children take part in dance and drumming contests. The winners get prizes.

Many powwows take place in the summer, but they also happen at other times of the year. They are held on reservations, at schools, universities, casinos, and other places. Some powwows are open to all people. Others are for Ojibwe people only.

This Ojibwe boy is dressed in special clothing worn at powwows.

Ojibwe people also come together to study their ancient language and traditions. They go to language classes, crafts workshops, traditional drumming sessions, and storytelling events. The Anishinabe language conference draws thousands of people each year. Members of the Ojibwe Language Society also work to keep the Ojibwe language and culture strong. The society is called Ojibwemowin Zagaswe'idiwin in the Ojibwe language.

The Ojibwe people have faced many challenges in their long history. Through the years, they have kept their ancient ways of life alive. They continue to carry their values, beliefs, and traditions into the future.

Modern Ojibwe act out how Ojibwe traders would approach a U.S. fort in the 1800s. One in the group drums to announce they are coming.

POPPED WILD RICE

This Ojibwe treat contains two traditional ingredients—
wild rice and maple syrup.

*2 to 3 tablespoons corn
oil or vegetable oil*

*1 cup hand-
processed wild rice*

¼ cup butter

*2 tablespoons maple
sugar or maple syrup*

salt

1. Place about ½ inch oil in a 12-inch, heavy skillet over medium heat.
2. Add the wild rice and swirl over medium heat until the kernels expand and pop.
3. Toss with butter, maple sugar or syrup, and salt.

Makes about 2 cups

PLACES TO VISIT

Fond du Lac Cultural Center and Museum

Cloquet, Minnesota

(218) 878-7582

http://fdlrez.com/Museum/index.htm

Visitors to this log cabin museum can learn about how Ojibwe people lived in the past as well as how they live in the present.

George W. Brown Jr. Ojibwe Museum and Cultural Center

Lac du Flambeau, Wisconsin

(715) 588-3333

http://www.ojibwe.com

This museum focuses on the customs, traditions, and arts of the Lac du Flambeau Band of Lake Superior Chippewa (Ojibwe) Indians. The museum also hosts powwows and classes on traditional Ojibwe crafts.

Mille Lacs Indian Museum

Onamia, Minnesota

(320) 532-3632

http://www.mnhs.org/places/sites/mlim/museum.html

This Ojibwe museum tells the story of the Mille Lacs Band of Ojibwe in central Minnesota. Exhibits include videos, interactive computer activities, listening stations, and historical objects. The museum also houses a crafts room where visitors can watch Ojibwe craftspeople at work.

Museum of Ojibwa Culture

Saint Ignace, Michigan

(906) 643-9161

http://www.stignace.com/attractions/ojibwa

Visitors to this museum can learn about life in the past on the Straits of Mackinac. Ojibwe and other American Indians first came to this part of Michigan hundreds of years ago.

GLOSSARY

band: a group of Ojibwe living together, usually in a village or several villages

chief: the leader of a group of Ojibwe

clan: a large group of families sharing common ancestors through the father's side

dodaim: the Ojibwe word for "clan"

Kitche Manitou: The Great Spirit, or God, in Ojibwe spirituality

manitou: a spirit being in Ojibwe spirituality

missionaries: people on a religious mission, generally to promote a particular type of religion. Missionaries in North America hoped to turn American Indians into Christians.

powwow: an American Indian ceremony

reservation: lands set aside for American Indians

self-determination: the ability of American Indian communities to take care of themselves

treaty: a written agreement between nations

wigwam: a traditional Ojibwe home made from a wooden frame covered with strips of birch bark

FURTHER READING

Erdrich, Louise. *The Birchbark House*. New York: Hyperion Books for Children, 1999. This novel tells the story of a seven-year-old Ojibwe girl living in the 1800s.

Regguinti, Gordon. *The Sacred Harvest: Ojibway Wild Rice Gathering*. Minneapolis: Lerner Publishing Company, 1992. This book describes the Ojibwe tradition of harvesting and using wild rice in modern times.

Van Laan, Nancy. *Shingebiss: An Ojibwe Legend*. Boston: Houghton Mifflin, 1997. In this Ojibwe story, a duck named Shingebiss must be brave and strong in order to outlast the winter.

Waboose, Jan Bourdeau. *Morning on the Lake*. Tonawanda, NY: Kids Can Press, 1997. In this story, an Ojibwe boy and his grandfather spend a day enjoying nature on a lake near their home.

Wittstock, Laura Waterman. *Ininatig's Gift of Sugar: Traditional Native Sugarmaking*. Minneapolis: Lerner Publishing Company, 1993. This book describes the Ojibwe tradition of making sugar from the syrup of maple trees in modern times.

WEBSITES

Mille Lacs Band of Ojibwe
http://www.millelacsojibwe.org
This website has information about Ojibwe history and culture and about the Mille Lacs Band of Ojibwe in Minnesota.

Ojibwemowin Zagaswe'idiwin
http://www.homepagedesign.biz/ojibwemowin
Run by the Ojibwe Language Society, this website offers information about Ojibwe history and culture. It also provides a helpful list of books, websites, and other resources.

Red Lake Nation
http://www.redlakenation.org
This official home page of Minnesota's Red Lake Ojibwe has links to
information on powwows at the reservation as well as a historical
overview of the Red Lake Nation.

White Earth Reservation
http://www.whiteearth.com
This website includes news, history, and cultural information on the
White Earth Nation of north-central Minnesota.

SELECTED BIBLIOGRAPHY

Danziger, Edmund Jefferson, Jr. *The Chippewas of Lake Superior*. Norman:
University of Oklahoma Press, 1978.

Johnston, Basil. *The Manitous: The Spiritual World of the Ojibway*. Saint Paul:
Minnesota Historical Society Press, 2001.

————. *Ojibway Ceremonies*. Lincoln: University of Nebraska Press, 1990.

————. *Ojibway Heritage*. New York: Columbia University Press, 1976.

Lund, Duane R. *The Lives and Times of Three Powerful Ojibwe Chiefs*.
Cambridge, MN: Adventure Publications, 2003.

"Ojibwe History." *Milwaukee Public Museum*. N.d.
http://www.mpm.edu/wirp/ICW-151.html (October 6, 2005).

Peacock, Thomas. *Ojibwe Waasa Inaabidaa: We Look in All Directions*. Afton,
MN: Afton Historical Society, 2002.

Treuer, Anton, ed. *Living Our Language: Ojibwe Tales and Oral Histories*. Saint
Paul: Minnesota Historical Society Press, 2001.

Warren, William W. *History of the Ojibway*. Saint Paul: Minnesota Historical
Society Press, 1984.

INDEX